THE OLD FASHIONED RAGGEDY ANN & ANDY ABC BOOK

PICTURES BY JOHNNY GRUELLE
VERSES BY ROBERT KRAUS
EDITED BY PAM KRAUS

Windmill Books / Simon & Schuster
New York

Illustrations © Copyright The Bobbs-Merrill Company, Inc. 1917, 1918,
1919, 1920, 1921, 1923, 1925, 1927, 1928,
1929, 1930, 1931, 1932, 1935, 1937, 1940,
1947, 1974, 1975
Text © Copyright Robert Kraus and Pamela Kraus 1981
Published by Windmill Books, Inc., and
Simon & Schuster, a Division of Gulf & Western Corporation
Simon & Schuster Building
1230 Avenue of the Americas
New York, New York 10020
Manufactured in the United States of America
10 9 8 7 6 5 4 3 2 1
ISBN 0-671-42552-8

Library of Congress Cataloging in Publication Data
Gruelle, Johnny, 1880?-1938.
The old-fashioned Raggedy Ann and Andy ABC book.
Summary: Rhyming stanzas introduce the letters of
the alphabet.
1. Alphabet rhymes. [1. Alphabet] I. Kraus,
Robert. II. Kraus, Pam. III. Title.
PZ8.3.G92801 1981   [E]   81-7500
ISBN 0-671-42552-8   AACR2

is for Ann
And Andy, too.
They've made this book
Just for you.

B is for Bed,
Good for a snooze.
Some beds sleep ones,
Some beds sleep twos.

C is for Crow,
His name is Bob.
Help him, please,
He needs a job.

D is for Dragon.
Andy's taking a ride,
But if I saw one
I'd surely hide.

E is for Elephant
With a trunk-y.
He likes to talk
To little monkeys.

F
is for Frog,
His name is Fred.
Isn't he cute
In his coat of red?

JOHNNY GRUELLE

G is for Gnome.
He sure is funny.
His favorite food
Is bread and honey.

H is for Horse
Going clippety-clop.
I can make him go,
But can I make him stop?

I is for Ice Cream.
It tastes so yummy,
And feels so good
Inside my tummy!

J

is for Jig,
A lively dance.
You can do it—
Come, take a chance!

K is for Kitty,
Soft and furry.
If you pet her,
She'll be purr-y.

L is for Little
House in a tree.
Too little for you,
Too little for me.

M is for Moon
Up in the sky.
How far is up?
How high is high?

N is for Nap,
Nice to take.
Dream a while
Before you wake.

O is for Owl.
They're very wise.
They wear glasses
On their eyes.

P is for Puppy.
I call him Spot.
I love my puppy
Quite a lot.

Q is for Quilt,
Warm and cozy,
When I'm feeling
Kind of dozy.

R is for Raggedy
Ann and Andy,
Sipping a soda,
Fine and dandy.

S is for Squirrel
High in a tree.
I'm looking at him,
He's looking at me.

T is for Tunnel
Dug by a mole.
Every tunnel
Starts with a hole!

U
is for Uncle
Who buys nice toys
To give to little
Girls and boys.

V is for Voyage
Out of the blue.
Bugs taking a trip
In a tiny canoe.

 is for Willie
Made of wood.
Sometimes he's bad,
Sometimes he's good.

X is for "X."
It comes before "Y."
You can make one
If you try.

Y is for Yellow,
My favorite color.
I find other
Colors duller.

Z is for a Zigzag
While on the run—
And now this ABC
Is done.

Goodbye for now.